Sun Power

Louis Capra

What helps plants grow?

Sun power!

Plants need sunlight
to grow.

What melts the ice?

7

Heat from the sun melts the ice.

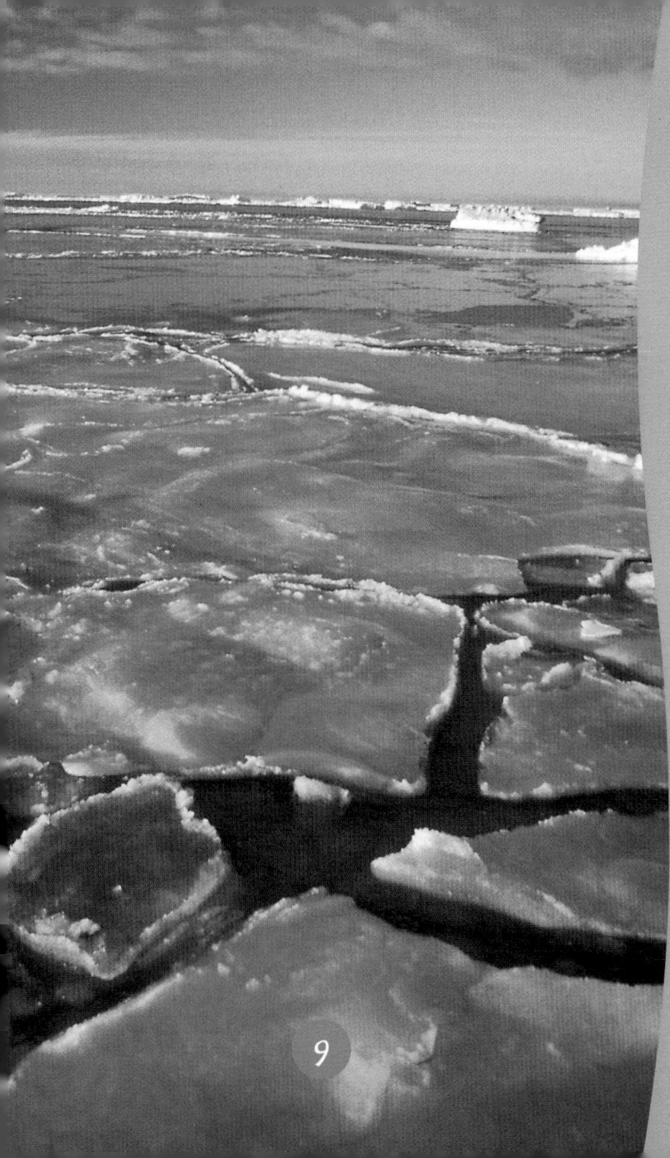

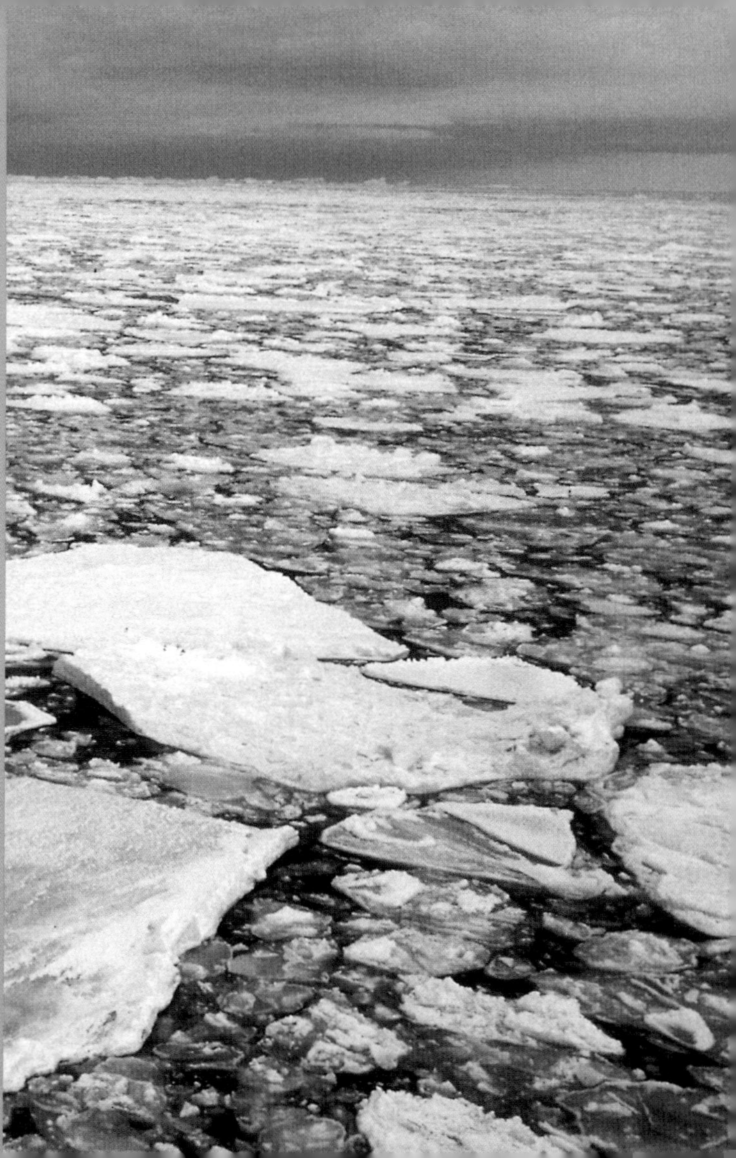

What makes this car go?

Sun power!

This car uses sunlight to make the car go.

13

What heats the houses?

Sun power!

The panels on the roofs use sunlight to heat the houses.

What helps dry the clothes?

Sun power!

Heat from the sun dries the clothes.

21

What helps keep you warm?

Sun power!

Index